You May Be Old If

You May Be Old If

by Douglas King

Day III Productions, Inc.

First published in the United States of America in 2021 by Day III Productions, Inc.
www.DayIIIProd.com

You May Be Old If copyright © 2021
Douglas King

All rights reserved. No part of this book may be reproduced, stored in a retrieval system or transmitted in any other form or by means electronic (including Internet websites), mechanical, photocopying, recording, or in any other form or by any means, without prior written permission from the publisher and copyright holder(s).

First Printing, September 2021
Printed in the USA
ISBN: 978-1-7376256-0-5

To my parents, Jack and Barbara,
who are old, really really old.
Unlike me, who is only half-way old

Introduction

You are holding a book. If you know what it is, you may be old.

I wrote this book because I was sick with Covid in 2021 and made a random comment to a friend after injuring myself. I said, "You know you're getting old when you pull a muscle having a bowel movement." I cleaned up the statement for this introduction (I also cleaned up after the bowel movement, in case you were wondering.) The comment struck me as funny and when my friend responded with laughter, I thought, *Hmmmm, I could be on to something here. I bet there are a lot of funny comments I could make about getting old.*

Never one to avoid a creative challenge, I set out to write as many simple, silly, surrealistic statements (can I use literation anymore in this sentence? (Oh, I guess I can!)) about getting old

– 7 –

that I could think of. Then, being the mercenary I am, I thought, *hey, I should publish these in a book and sell it!* (Yes, I think a lot to myself. Wait. Who else would I be thinking to? Never mind, that's a rabbit trail that only old people would follow. Let's stay on track.)

There you have it. That is the genesis of the book you hold in your hand which makes a perfect introduction for what you are about to experience. Have fun. Read a couple of comments a day. Don't rush, unless you really are that old and you don't know if you will be around in a few days. Then, by all means, read this book from cover to cover as fast as you can.

They say laughter is the best medicine. I hope so. I also hope you laugh at what's to come. That's the point, purpose, principle, and proposition of this project. (I really do enjoy good literation. Can you tell?) If you're easily offended, you may want to put this book down and go drink an Ensure, because I am sure there will be something in these pages to offend you. But it's all in good fun. We all get old, we can't avoid it, so we might as well laugh about it.

*"Life is like a roll of toilet paper.
The closer you get to the end,
the faster it goes."*
~ Anonymous

You may be old if ...

You pull a muscle by having
a bowel movement.

"Old age isn't so bad if you consider the alternative."
~Maurice Chevalier

You may be old if ...

Bending over to tie your shoe is considered exercise.

"By the time you're 80 years old you've learned everything. You only have to remember it."
~ George Burns

You may be old if ...

What was I talking about?

You may be old if ...

You spend half an hour trying to explain what a phone book is to a teenager, and they still look at you like you're insane.

You waited fifteen minutes for your cell phone to have a dial tone before you tried making a call.

You may be old if ...

When you cough you worry your teeth may fall out.

You think milk only
comes from cows.

"A man is a fool if he drinks before he reaches the age of 50, and a fool if he doesn't afterward."
~ Frank Lloyd Wright

You may be old if ...

The munchies you get after smoking a joint are for prunes and Metamucil biscuits.

You may be old if ...

The redwoods of California were just saplings when you were five years old.

You blow your nose and something unexpectantly comes out the other end of your body.

"One can't believe impossible things. I dare say you haven't had much practice," said the Queen. "When I was your age, I always did it for half-an-hour a day. Why, sometimes I've believed as many as six impossible things before breakfast."
~ Lewis Carroll

You may be old if ...

Just driving to the corner store is an all-day adventure.

"Old age is an excellent time for outrage. My goal is to say or do at least one outrageous thing every week."
~ Maggie Kuhn

You may be old if ...

Getting one thing done a day
and remembering what it was is a
major accomplishment.

"I don't feel old. I don't feel anything until noon. Then it's time for my nap."
~ Bob Hope

You may be old if ...

You automatically groan every time you sit down or stand up from a chair.

You may be old if ...

Standing up elicits more groans
and snorts than a post-game
pro football team.

Every time you sit down it seems like a good time for a nap.

*"Age is an issue of mind over matter.
If you don't mind, it doesn't matter."*
~ Mark Twain

You may be old if ...

Your daily pill box gets
exponentially larger every year.

"Old age is always fifteen years older than I am."
~ Oliver Wendell Holmes

You may be old if ...

Guessing which body parts will ache on any given day is like playing bingo!

You may be old if ...

The number of times you get up at night to go to the bathroom is equal to the number of fingers and toes you have.

The word "depends" is a clothing option.

"I feel about aging the way William Saroyan said he felt about death: 'Everybody has to do it,' but I always believed an exception would be made in my case."
~ Martha Beck

You may be old if ...

You begin most of your conversations with, "When I was your age…"

"Some guy said to me: 'Don't you think you're too old to sing rock n roll?' I said: 'You'd better check with Mick Jagger.'"
~ Cher

You may be old if ...

Classical music means The Beatles,
The Rolling Stones, and The Who.

You may be old if ...

You have multiple pairs of reading glasses, of varying strength, in each room of the house, and you still can't find a pair.

Often a fart is more than
just a fart.

"It's paradoxical that the idea of living a long life appeals to everyone, but the idea of getting old doesn't appeal to anyone."
~ Andy Rooney

You may be old if ...

Your friends greet you each time by saying, "You're still alive?"

You may be old if ...

Reruns on TV seem new to you.

You have so many doctor's appointments they've begun to feel like dates.

You may be old if ...

A night on the town means picking up your prescriptions and fast food.

You somehow injure yourself just sleeping at night.

You may be old if...

You have a standing reservation at the local buffet.

"Dinner and a movie" begin at 4 pm and is over by 7 pm.

"My experience is that as soon as people are old enough to know better, they don't know anything at all."
~ Oscar Wilde

You may be old if ...

You need reading glasses and a magnifying glass to read the print on medicine bottles and cooking instructions on food boxes.

"It is a good idea to obey all the rules when you're young just so you'll have the strength to break them when you're old."
~ Mark Twain

You may be old if ...

You think you're driving too fast,
and you aren't even doing
the speed limit.

You may be old if ...

You try using your cell phone to change the channels on your television.

Getting out of bed requires so much energy you immediately need a nap.

"Age is not a particularly interesting subject. Anyone can get old. All you have to do is live long enough."
~ Groucho Marx

You may be old if ...

You still read a paper *TV Guide* and are proud of that fact.

You may be old if ...

Taking a nap is literally written on
your schedule for every day
at 4 o'clock.

You print the directions from MapQuest.

"I'm very pleased to be here. Let's face it, at my age I'm very pleased to be anywhere."
~ George Burns

You may be old if ...

Sitting, just sitting, becomes your main activity for the day.

You may be old if ...

You actually use cash to buy stuff and do your best to provide the exact change for every purchase.

You look forward to your annual colonoscopy, so you finally have a selfie to show your kids.

"Old people love to give good advice to console themselves for no longer being able to set a bad example."
~ Francois de la Rochefoucauld

You may be old if ...

No one understands the
pop-culture references
you make anymore.

You may be old if ...

Door-to-door salesmen and telemarketers actually try to hang up or close the door on you to get you to stop telling them all about your kids and grandkids.

You sprain your finger jabbing at the virtual buttons on your smartphone screen.

"You can live to be a hundred if you give up all things that make you want to live to be a hundred."
~ Woody Allen

You may be old if ...

You eat anything you damn well want regardless of the ramifications because you've lived long enough to deserve it.

You may be old if ...

Instead of reading car and boat magazines, you have a subscription to coffin and urn catalogs.

Every time you go to the grocery store you say, "When did everything get so expensive?"

"A lady of a 'certain age,' which means certainly aged."
~ Lord George Byron

You may be old if ...

A "hot" chick means a menopausal woman having hot flashes.

You may be old if ...

You not only forget why you enter a room; you forget what room you walked into.

Dressing up for dinner means you wear pants to the dinner table.

You may be old if ...

You consider "late night" to mean any time after 6 pm.

Reading a novel takes longer because of all the spontaneous naps.

*"You are only young once, but
you can stay immature indefinitely."*
~ Ogden Nash

You may be old if …

Eating ice cream after every meal, including breakfast, seems like a good thing to do, because, why the hell not?

You may be old if ...

Your 401K should really just be called 401OK.

Your lifetime membership
at the gym expires.

You may be old if ...

You use Poligrip to glue everything in the house that breaks.

You sneeze and throw out
your back.

You may be old if...

Your doctor offers to make house calls because she saves the time it takes for you to walk to the exam room and climb up on the table.

Hair no longer grows on your head or shins, but has sprouted out of your ears, off your shoulders, at random areas on your back, and what the hell is happening with your eyebrows?

You may be old if ...

You realize you need dusting because you haven't moved off the sofa in nearly a week.

You eat dessert first because you never know if you'll make it through the actual meal.

You may be old if ...

You've actually considered using your clothing steamer on your skin to get the wrinkles out.

Getting a haircut actually means
getting your one and only hair cut.

You may be old if ...

You'd rather drink an Ensure protein shake rather than expend the energy to chew your dinner.

You have more hair in your left nostril than on your head.

"At age 20, we worry about what others think of us. At age 40, we don't care what they think of us. At age 60, we discover they haven't been thinking of us at all."
~ Ann Landers

You may be old if ...

The only time people want your signature is on Power of Attorney documents.

You may be old if ...

You actually enjoy playing canasta, and even know what it is in the first place.

Your social security number only has six digits and begins with zero.

"People ask me what I'd most appreciate getting for my eighty-seventh birthday. I tell them, a paternity suit."
~ George Burns

You may be old if ...

You yell "Bingo" to celebrate having a successful trip to the bathroom, or an orgasm.

You may be old if ...

You've lived long enough that the bubble gum you swallowed when you were eight has finally passed through your colon.

Your workout routine consists
of getting out of bed.
That's it.

You may be old if ...

You outlived your pet Galapagos tortoise.

The Hawaiian shirt you love
wearing has come back in style…
five times.

You may be old if ...

Your refrigerator is covered in so many magnets your pacemaker malfunctions when you go to grab a Jell-O snack pack.

Wine made the year you were born is considered well-aged and sells for over $10,000 a bottle.

You may be old if ...

You think Burning Man is a guy with a venereal disease.

It's 3 pm and...
Zzzzzzzzzzzzzzzzzzzzzzzzzz

You may be old if ...

Getting a 10% discount at every restaurant you dine at is worth fighting a waiter to the death for.

A paper cut could kill you because of all the blood thinner medicine you take.

"Time may be a great healer, but it is a lousy beautician."
~ Anonymous

You may be old if ...

You've given up on your looks and are only concern about how you smell.

You may be old if ...

You think the electric cart at the grocery store goes too fast.

Black socks, sandals, and cargo shorts, with a fanny pack, is acceptable to wear in public.

"Talking is the disease of age."
~ Ben Johnson

You may be old if ...

You honestly believe the clerk at the grocery store and the waiter at the restaurant care what job your son has, what state he lives in, and what his relationship status is.

"A stockbroker urged me to buy a stock that would triple its value every year. I told him, 'At my age, I don't even buy green bananas.'"
– Claude Pepper

You may be old if ...

You can pass an entire day
just wrapping coins.

"For the first half of your life, people tell you what you should do; for the second half, they tell you what you should have done."
~ Richard J. Needham

You may be old if ...

You can make a McDonalds Big Mac and fries last for three meals.

"I don't do drink or drugs. At my age, I get the same effect just standing up too fast."
~Unknown

You may be old if ...

You could get more done if you didn't sleep 20 hours a day.

*"I don't plan to grow old gracefully.
I plan to have face-lifts
until my ears meet."*
~ Rita Rudner

You may be old if ...

You're often mistaken for a turtle
because your skin is leathery,
you move slow, you eat salad,
and you are generally happy.

*"We don't grow older,
we grow riper."*
~ Pablo Picasso

You may be old if ...

When shopping for cantaloupe
you are reminded of your prostate.

"Today is the oldest you've ever been, and the youngest you'll ever be again."
~ Eleanor Roosevelt

You may be old if …

The only thing you can get up the energy to do is to watch TV.

"I don't let my age define me but the side-effects are getting harder to ignore."
~ Unknown

You may be old if ...

Walking up a flight of stairs takes all day.

"Middle age is when you're sitting at home on a Saturday night and the telephone rings and you hope it isn't for you."
~ Ogden Nash

You may be old if ...

You tried to "get down" on the dance floor but only managed to fall down and now you can't get back up.

"The secret of staying young is to live honestly, eat slowly and lie about your age."
~ Lucille Ball

You may be old if …

You spend more time shaving your ears than you do your face.

*"Respect old people.
They graduated from school without
Google or Wikipedia."*
~ Unknown

You may be old if ...

The only student debt you have to worry about is when you pay Geek Squad to teach you how to use Google and Outlook.

"People say that age is just a state of mind. I say it's more about the state of your body."
~ Geoffrey Parfitt

You may be old if ...

As a man, you've found some benefit to peeing sitting down.

"Middle age is when a guy starts turning off lights for economic rather than romantic reasons."
~Eli Cass

You may be old if ...

The highlight of your day is
getting and opening the mail.

You may be old if ...

If you were a car, your odometer would have reset to 00000000.

You can't remember the last decade you celebrated Mother's or Father's Day for your parents.

"How old would you be if you didn't know how old you was?"
~ Satchel Paige

You may be old if ...

You can't calculate how old you'd be in dog years without using a calculator.

"Beware of the young doctor and the old barber."
~Benjamin Franklin

You may be old if …

Your doctor tells you not to worry about taking the time to visit for your annual check-up anymore.

"As you get older, the pickings get slimmer, but the people don't."
– Carrie Fisher

You may be old if ...

You outlived 45 pet hamsters.

"Old age is no place for sissies."
~ Bette Davis

You may be old if ...

Congratulations,
you may get to see
Haley's comet...
a third time.

"As we grow older, our bodies get shorter and our anecdotes longer."
– Robert Quillen

You may be old if …

You find many of your conversations focus on the subject of the frequency and size of your bowel movements.
This is considered an acceptable and interesting topic of conversation.

"Birthdays are good for you. Statistics show that the people who have the most live the longest."
~ Larry Lorenzoni

You may be old if ...

The fire department waits on standby when they light the candles on your birthday cake.

You may be old if ...

You've had to make "lifelong friends" three times.

You visited Egypt and the locals tried to wrap you in linen cloth and stuff you in a tomb.

"Age is no guarantee of maturity."
~ Lawana Blackwell

You may be old if …

All wine and cheese are
younger than you.

*"At my age I've heard it all;
I've seen it all; and I've done it all.
I just can't remember it at all."*
~Unknown

You may be old if ...

Historians call you for information.

"If I had known I was going to live this long, I'd have taken better care of myself."
~ Anonymous

You may be old if ...

The mortician calls you each week
to check on you.

You may be old if ...

You have to wear three media alert bracelets to include all your conditions.

Instead of Facebook, you read the obituary page to keep up with friends.

You may be old if ...

You play connect the dots with the age spots on your hand and come up with something new each week.

You ask for a senior discount everywhere you go, even at the funeral home.

You may be old if …

You don't play tennis, but you keep a stash of tennis balls for your walker.

You've celebrated so many Thanksgivings and Christmases, you feel like you've committed a form of genocide against turkeys and pigs.

"I will never be an old man. To me, old age is always 15 years older than I am."
~ Francis Bacon

You may be old if …

Your "senior moment" last 24/7.

"I've reached the age where my brain went from "You probably shouldn't say that" to "What the hell, let's see what happens."
~ Unknown

You may be old if …

You still read physical books
like this one.
(Thank you!)

www.ingramcontent.com/pod-product-compliance
Lightning Source LLC
Chambersburg PA
CBHW030908080526
44589CB00010B/206